Time Zones Around the World

by Adam McClellan

Scott Foresman
is an imprint of

Glenview, Illinois • Boston, Massachusetts • Mesa, Arizona
Shoreview, Minnesota • Upper Saddle River, New Jersey

Every effort has been made to secure permission and provide appropriate credit for photographic material. The publisher deeply regrets any omission and pledges to correct errors called to its attention in subsequent editions.

Unless otherwise acknowledged, all photographs are the property of Pearson.

Photo locations denoted as follows: Top (T), Center (C), Bottom (B), Left (L), Right (R), Background (Bkgd)

Opener Corbis; 1 (TL) ©Alan Schein Photography/Corbis, 1 (TR) ©Michael S. Yamashita/Corbis, 1 (BL) ©Jeffrey L. Rotman/Corbis, 1 (BR) ©Paul Almasy/Corbis; 6 ©Bettmann/Corbis; 14 ©Alan Schein Photography/Corbis; 15 ©Paul Almasy/Corbis; 17 ©Gabe Palmer/Corbis; 18 (T) ©Joseph Sohm; ChromoSohm Inc./Corbis, 18 (B) ©Reuters/Corbis; 19 (TR) ©Owen Franken/Corbis, 19 (CL) ©Charles & Josette Lenars/Corbis, 19 (BR) ©Jeffrey L. Rotman/Corbis; 20 (TR) ©Michael S. Yamashita/Corbis, 20 (BR) ©Charles O'Rear/Corbis; 21 ©Roger Ressmeyer/Corbis

ISBN 13: 978-0-328-39459-3
ISBN 10:   0-328-39459-9

1 2 3 4 5 6 7 8 9 10 V0G1 17 16 15 14 13 12 11 10 09 08

CONTENTS

Chapter 1
Measuring Time

How do you tell time? You look at a clock, of course!

But what clock? Where? How do you tell what time it is across the United States? What about across the ocean, or on the other side of the world? Telling time can take a little more work than just glancing at the clock on the wall.

Before we can discuss time around the world, we need to understand how time is measured. We measure time in two ways, by the year and by the day. A year is the time it takes the Earth to make one trip around the sun. That is 365 days plus six hours. The extra hours add a day to the calendar every four years (Leap Year).

The day is measured by the time it takes the Earth to complete one **rotation** on its axis, 24 hours.

Natural Time

Think about how a day would look if you lived in the wilderness, without a clock. The first thing you would see in the morning would be sunrise, when the sun rises above the **horizon** in the east. Then the sun slowly makes its way across the sky,

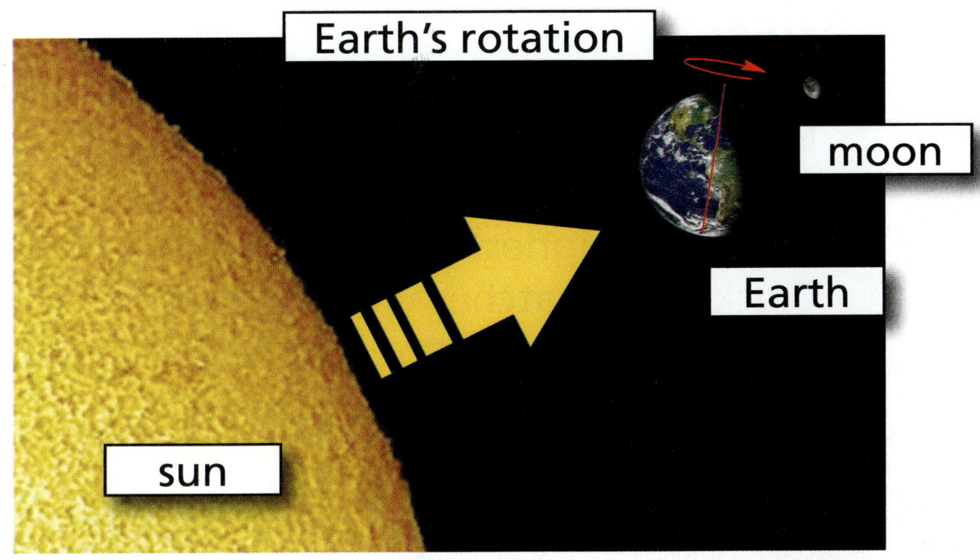

until it sinks into the western horizon at sunset.

The sun seems to travel across the sky because of the rotation of the Earth. The sun's rays light up only part of the Earth at any given time. The rest of the Earth is dark. And as the Earth spins, part of it is brought into the light of day and part into the darkness of night.

Because of this action, it wouldn't make much sense to have everyone's clocks set to the exact same time. Imagine if the world was on the same time, then night and day would come at very different times, depending on where you lived in the world. The sun would rise at 6:30 A.M. in some places but at 10:00 P.M. in others!

Chapter 2
The Birth of Time Zones

Many years ago, each town kept its own time, based on **solar time**. Noon marked the sun at its highest point overhead.

Clocks and watches weren't very **accurate** back then, so people often chose a special clock in each town to tell the official time.

Different towns would have noon at different times of the day. This meant that their other clock times would be different too. What was 9:20 A.M. to one town might be 9:23 A.M. to another town down the road. For a long time, that worked just fine, as most people didn't travel very much.

In the 1800s, however, the growing use of the railroads changed everything! Trains made travel from town to town much quicker. A trip that once took a week could now be made by train in a day.

Train schedules made people think about time. Each railroad line set its schedule based on its home city. As a train got farther and farther into its trip, the time on the train became more and more varied from the time at each station. A Philadelphia train might be scheduled to arrive in Pittsburgh at 5:00 P.M. But according to Pittsburgh time, it was only 4:40 P.M. If you didn't know the difference, you could miss your train!

Eventually, train stations would have many different clocks on their walls, each one set to a different train's time. Something had to be done to make it easier to tell time in different places.

In 1883, the railroads in the United States agreed to divide the country into four **standard** time zones: Eastern, Central, Mountain, and Pacific. All the cities and towns in each zone would share the exact same time.

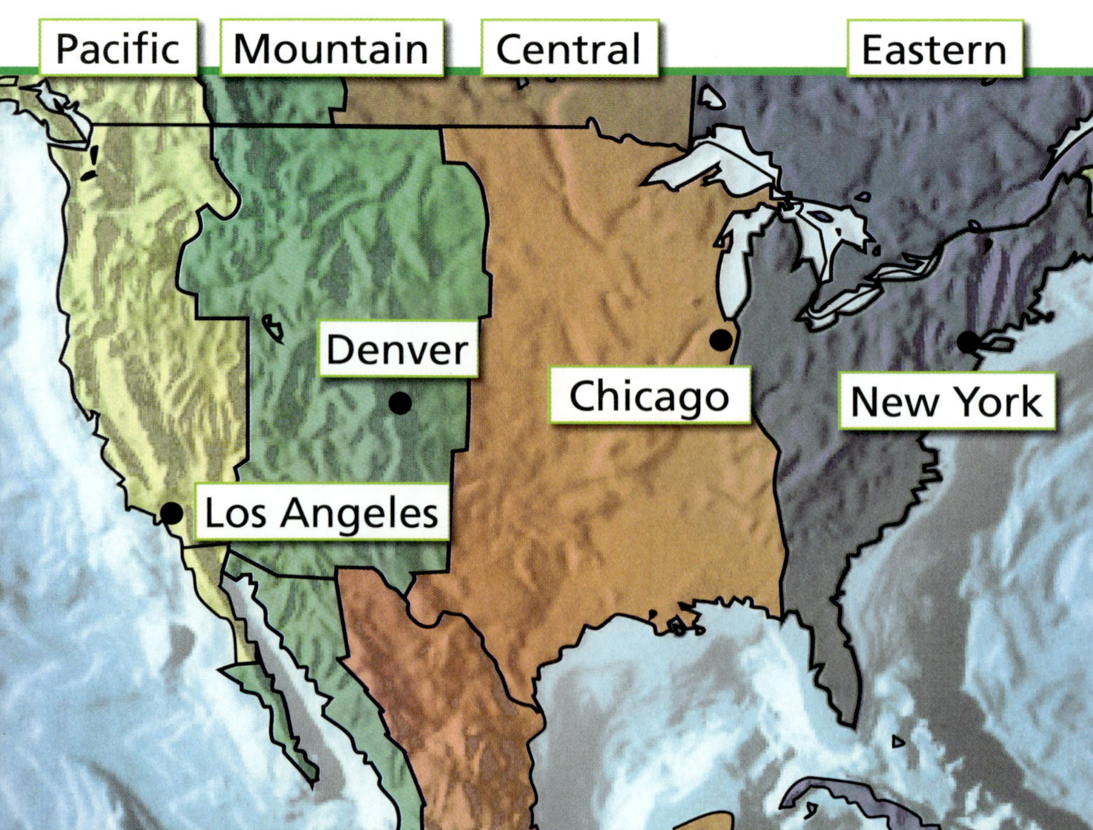

People from twenty-five countries met at a **conference** in Washington, D.C., to solve the problem of telling time around the world.

At the conference, the group decided to divide the world into twenty-four equal time zones, represented by 15° of longitude. The time in each zone would be based on adding or subtracting hours from the time in the town of Greenwich, England (Greenwich Mean Time, now called Coordinated Universal Time). The conference chose Greenwich because it had an **observatory** that kept accurate information on the Earth's rotation. For the first time, people had a simple way of knowing what time it was anywhere in the world!

Chapter 3
Time Zones Today

In the original plan, the lines between time zones would run straight north and south. But things didn't quite work out that way!

Part of the reason this plan didn't work out was that people in each country were able to choose how to set the country's time. South Korea, which is a small country, was split in half by one of the original time

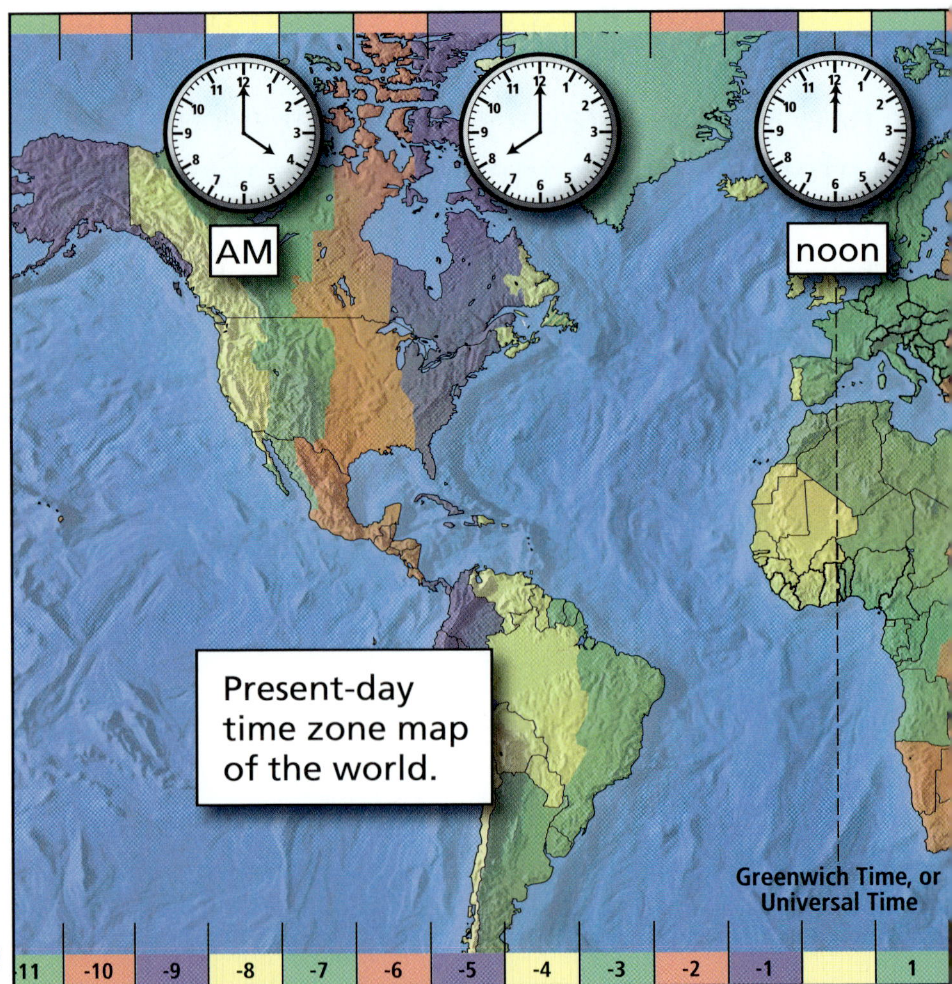

Present-day time zone map of the world.

zone lines, so instead of dealing with two times for the country, the South Koreans moved the time zone line to the west. That way, all South Koreans would set their watches to the same time.

The same thing happened in the United States. Some states moved the time zone boundaries in one direction or another so that the whole state would be in a single zone. Other states seem to be perfectly fine with being split into two time zones.

What all this means is that instead of running straight up and down on a map, the world's time zones are in more of a zigzag pattern from north to south.

How to Use a Time Zone Map

Our time zone map may be more confusing today than it was back in 1884. But it still allows us to see what time it is anywhere in the world. Let's look at how the time zone map works.

First, find where you live on the time zone map. Then write down the time. To figure out what time it is in the zones to your west, subtract one hour for each time zone you cross. For the zones to your east, add one hour for each time zone.

For example, say it's 5:30 P.M. in Atlanta, and you want to know the time in London, England. To get from Atlanta to London, you cross five time zones going east. That means you add five hours to 5:30 P.M., showing you that it's 10:30 P.M. in London—getting toward most people's bedtime.

Chapter 4
Time Zone Facts

- It makes sense that the biggest country in the world would have the most time zones. Russia has ten time zones in all!

- China should be split into five different time zones. The Chinese government, however, chooses to have the whole country run on the time of the capital city, Beijing. That means that the sun may not set in the western part of the country until after 10:00 P.M.! Not only that, but people crossing the **border** into China from Kazakhstan must set their watches ahead by two whole hours.

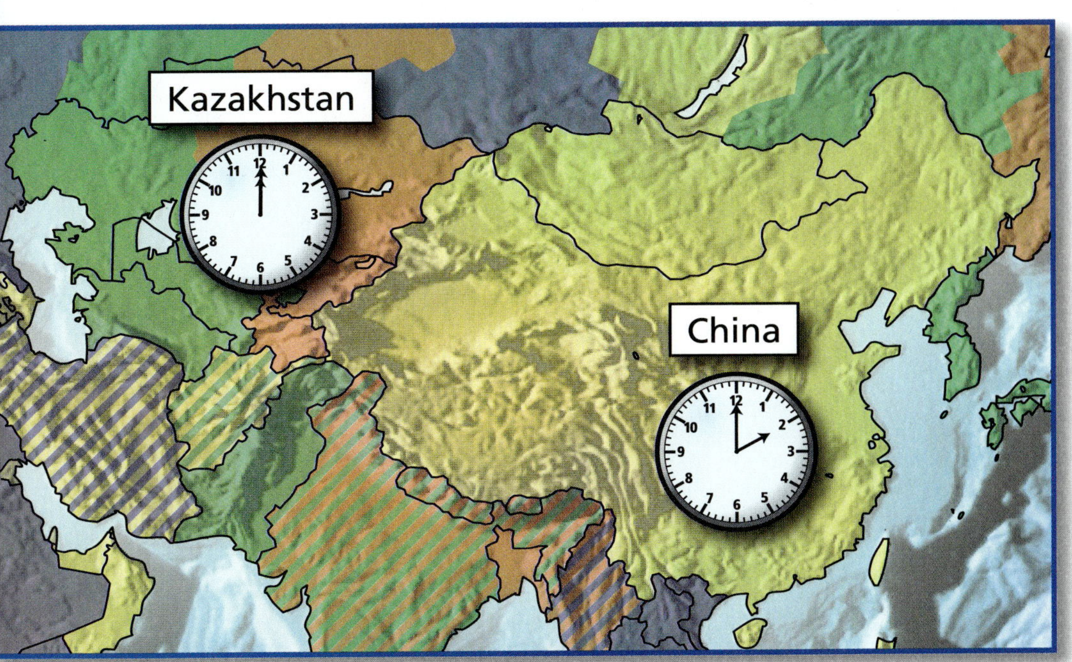

- The time zone with the fewest people is probably the tiny frozen islands of South Georgia in the middle of the Atlantic Ocean.

- Some countries, like India and Iran, set their time to be different by a half hour instead of a full hour. The country of Nepal makes things even more complicated and sets its clocks fifteen minutes earlier than everyone else in its time zone.

- If you travel fast enough from east to west, you can get to a place "earlier" than when you left! Suppose you are

returning to New York from London. You will have to cross five east-to-west time zones, which means that you subtract five hours from London time on your way to New York. A very fast plane makes the trip in about three and a half hours. So when you get to New York, it is an hour and a half earlier than when you left London!

- The United States has seven time zones in all (Eastern, Central, Mountain, Pacific, Alaskan, Hawaii-Aleutians, and Samoans).

Chapter 5
The International Date Line

There's another important "time line" on the Earth's map, the International Date Line. "International" means something that involves many different nations. This isn't just a time-zone boundary. When you cross the International Date Line, you move a whole day in time!

There's a very good reason for the International Date Line, and it goes back to the fact that the Earth is round. As you know, if you cross time zones heading east, you move ahead an hour for each time zone, and if you cross them heading west, you move back an hour.

Now suppose that two people in Chicago are looking at a globe. It's 7:20 on Wednesday evening, and they're trying to figure out what time it is in Bangladesh, on the other side of the world, twelve time zones away. One person counts the time zones going east and the other one counts them going west. They both end up in Bangladesh, but one person thinks it's 7:20 on Thursday morning there, and the other says it's actually 7:20 on Wednesday morning. Who's right? Well, without an

International Date Line, we couldn't really know. The International Date Line keeps it simple, however. If you cross it going west, you add a day, and if you cross it going east, you subtract a day.

The International Date Line runs through the middle of the Pacific Ocean. (See the map on pages 10–11.) So, in the example here, the person who was counting time zones going west from Chicago was the person who crossed the International Date Line. They need to add a day to their **calculations** to get the right answer: in Bangladesh, it's 7:20 on Thursday morning.

Chapter 6
Around the World in a Minute

So you think you're getting the hang of time zones? Let's take a quick trip around the world.

Our first stop is Los Angeles, where it's 6:33 A.M. Friday morning, Pacific Time.

The sun is rising, and some people are getting out of bed or eating a bowl of cereal. Others are already on the way to their jobs. The day is just beginning.

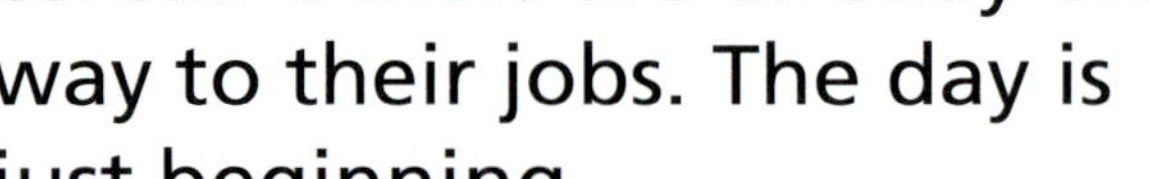

In New York City, the time is 9:33 A.M., Eastern Standard Time. Most children are already in school, and millions of people are just settling down to their jobs. On Wall Street,

the bell that starts the New York Stock Exchange was rung a few minutes ago. Traders are busy trying to buy and sell stocks.

Across the ocean, it's 3:33 P.M., Central European Time in Rome, Italy. School has let out for the day, and children stroll home. Most grown-ups are still at work though— at least for another hour or so.

A little farther east, the time in Cairo, Egypt, is 4:33 P.M. The sun is on its way down, but the air is still hot. The streets are filled with cars. Later, as the sun sinks even lower in the sky, people will go out to enjoy the cool of evening.

It's 8:03 P.M. in Mumbai, India. As night falls, a movie director and his crew finish their day of filming.

Thousands of colorful lights brighten up downtown Tokyo, where it's 11:33 P.M. Almost all the children are in bed. Some grown-ups are still out, having a late meal, or going to a show.

In the middle of the Pacific Ocean, it's 2:33 on Saturday morning in the small island country of Fiji. By this time of night, most people have gone to sleep.

A little farther east, it's 4:33 A.M. in Hawaii. Everyone's asleep here, too, but it's Friday morning—we crossed the International Date Line coming from Fiji! People here are about to experience the day you just saw in the rest of the world.

From Hawaii, it's just another two time zones more to the east to get to Los Angeles, where it's still 6:33 A.M. on Friday.

Back Where You Started

You're back! But you get an idea of just how confusing travel would be if each city still set its own time! Figuring out the time on the other side of the world may not be as easy as just checking your watch. With a clock, a map, and a little math, however, you can come up with the answer in almost no time at all!

Time Zone Travel

Calling all world travelers! Time Zone Airlines is now selling tickets to fly anywhere in the world. Each ticket includes three cities: one to start from and the other two to arrive at.

Ticket agents for Time Zone Airlines have a very important job. They have to be sure that each ticket includes an itinerary, a short schedule that tells passengers when their planes take off and land. After all, your passengers don't want to miss their flights, right?

1. Pair up with one of your classmates. Then choose roles: one of you will be the passenger and the other will be the ticket agent.

2. The flight you are writing an itinerary for starts from where you live (or the city with the nearest airport). The passenger can look at a map of the world to choose the other two cities.

3. The ticket agent can use a ruler and the map's scale to figure out the distance between the first city and the second city and between the second city and the third city. Write each distance down.

4. Time Zone Airline jets fly at 500 miles per hour. Work together to figure out how long each flight will take.

5. Have the ticket agent write out an itinerary. The itinerary should list the cities for each flight, along with the times that the plane leaves one city and arrives in the next city. Be sure to check the time-zone map on pages 10 and 11.

Glossary

accurate *adj.* correct.

border *n.* a line that officially separates countries or regions.

calculations *n.* the process or steps used to work out the answers to mathematical problems.

conference *n.* a meeting to discuss serious matters.

horizon *n.* a line where the land and sea seem to meet the sky.

observatory *n.* a place where scientists watch and study the stars, planets, weather, earthquakes, etc.

rotation *n.* a spinning around on a central point.

solar time *n.* the time of day as figured out by using the sun as a guide.

standard *n.* something that people agree to accept as accurate or true.